Flabbermouth Moments

Flabbergasted plus Foot in Mouth

By Christine Hannon

Dedication

Flabbermouth is my word for 'foot in mouth' moments that leaves one 'flabbergasted'. These are true events that have happened in my life over the past 50 years. I hope you enjoy reading them and at least get a chuckle. In some cases those who know me personally may find they bring back a memory or two.

I would like to thank my husband, children, grandchildren and friends for supplying me with the ammunition for these short stories.

I referred to these stories as my 'Flabbermouth' Moments. I am the 'Queen of flabbermouth' .I was always saying something at the wrong time or in the wrong place, making me the unpaid clown who made everyone else laugh.

My kids would often say, "Oh it is just one of mom's 'Flabbermouth Moments' again."

The sad part for me, but the entertaining part for my family and friends, was that I didn't realize what I had said until it was pointed out to me. Then even I couldn't believe it. Poor Ron would just shake his head in embarrassment or disbelief. One would think after so many years he would get used to it right? Wrong.

Here are some of those moments.

Chapter Fourteen: Nuns Bean Embarrassed

Chapter One: Squid anyone?

I love to cook and experiment with many different foods. Each one of my family members has their favorite dish and on this particular night it was Ron's turn to choose. –Breaded deep fried squid. Yuk! As much as I didn't like the cleaning, the cutting, or the feel or look of these ugly sea creatures but I sucked it up and did the dirty deed. I would make Ron his favorite, no matter what the 'yukkies' did to me.

The kids teased me saying that the tentacles looked like baby spiders. So that didn't help the situation in the least. I detested any form of creepy, crawly things. Passionately, I cleaned and then cut (perfect sized rings) and then I floured, battered, and fried those ghastly looking morsels. All the time working with my nose turned up. Every so often I took the time to remind him how much I must love him, to do this wonderful thing just for him.

Now, came the moment of truth, the taste test. Was all my hard work up to par? I structured the freshly deep fried squid on a lovely, white, platter with the perfect condiments, ready for him to indulge. If I must say so myself it was a very tempting looking dish.

The kids each started to dig in, when Douglas said, "Dad, don't the tentacles look like spiders?"

Annoyingly, I told him to stop talking and eat. I gave a deep rooted cold shudder. Ron looked over at him and smiled it was the most devilish smile I have seen in a while. Winking at the kids, Ron picked up one of the tentacles and placed it dangling out of the left corner of his mouth. He proceeded to chase me around the house and out into the yard. As I frantically ran from him, I was squealing for him to stop.

My neighbor Deloris, who was outside watering her lawn, hollered to me, "Why are you squealing?"

Out of breath, pointing and gasping I said, "Ron is chasing me with his testicles in his mouth."

With a coy surprised look on her face she said, "Oh my how extremely talented he is." She laughed so hard I was sure her sides would split.

Before long, there was a rumour going around the neighborhood about just how gifted my husband was. I was lovingly tormented for a very long time. Some snickered and one friend even made a comment about squid being on sale at the local fish market. All the teasing was in jest and I was able to laugh too. I however would never live this one down, as my children now grown, still tease me.

Chapter Two: For Your Own Health

Sometimes remembering the Flabbermouth moments are downright painful. This is especially true when I remember just how dumb I really sounded. In some cases, it takes a few minutes to really sink in. Remember the reference from another story, about my not being the brightest bulb on the tree? This was one of those occasions. I however cannot believe my family still has it locked in their memory banks. Somehow they cannot remember my birthday but *this* they have burned deep into their brains.

The family and I were sitting on the couch watching a science, health show one evening on t.v. The discussion was about how individual parts of the body function and move. The first part of the program was based on the problems and functions of our joints.

The second part of the program discussed the damage that could be done by smoking and what it does to the organs and growth hormones. I found all of this rather interesting and it had me deep in thought. At the time Ron was a smoker so I was taking it all in. I on the other hand had never parted my lips for the deadly cancer stick. In my mind part of getting Ron to quit smoking might be found in this newly acquired knowledge. When the first part of the show was over, Ron noticed I was staring at him intensely.

"What on earth are you staring at?" He said with a rather inquisitive look on his face.

"I was just thinking."

"Oh my, not again?"

"Yes again, the show has made me think." With that, he rolled his eyes and the kids laughed.

"Oh no, mom is thinking again," piped up one of our rug rats.

Now I was determined to show them I could say something intelligent. So out it came.

"Honey, I want to be serious now okay? " Ron nodded as I spoke. "When we talk, what jaw moves our top or our bottom one?"

"You are kidding right?" Ron questioned with a furrowed brow.

"No." I was annoyed that he would put it that way.

Then as if the family had rehearsed the response for weeks they in unison started talking. Moving their heads up and down, pushing their heads back trying to keep their bottom jaw still. They were laughing so hard they almost rolled on the floor.

"Any more questions, dear? Does anyone have anything to say to your mom?"

Hysterically one after the other they teased me unmercifully. I soon saw the humor in the latest Flabbermouth moment.

That night when we went to bed Ron apologized for being so hard on me as he said. "Honey you must admit it was pretty darn funny."

"I know it was." I said embarrassed but still able to laugh. And then, Flabbermouth struck again, "At least I didn't tell you I was worried about smoking stunting your growth."

With that, Ron reached over and patted me on my head and as I turned to face him, I saw his arm pulled up inside his shirt showing only his hand, wiggling his fingers at me. He was by now laughing so hard the bed was shaking. I slapped him on the arm and rolled over turning my back to him. I was trying extremely hard to restrain myself so as not to laugh out loud myself. He was right though it was really darn funny.

Chapter Three: Cremation Anyone?

I wasn't going to share this story with anyone today with Christmas being so close, but I think it might be a positive thing. My friend Cheryl just called to tell me she is still laughing and doesn't think she will stop anytime soon.

Cheryl came for a Christmas coffee this evening. She noticed the card on the fireplace that I had received from our vet that had our late Cercie's kitty footprint on it. We soon found ourselves talking about our furry family members who had passed away. We discussed how we felt about them leaving us far too soon. I talked about my 19 year old 'Cercie' and she talked about her canine friend 'Wishbone.' I soon teared up after just a few moments into our conversation. Especially when I remembered how she buried her weary head in my bosom, while the vet relieved her of her unbearable pain.

Cheryl asked, "Did you have her cremated to keep her?"

"No, we just had her paw print made. It is preserved on that plaque on the fireplace."

"I can handle almost anything, accept cremation." She added with a shudder, "I had to watch a movie on it for nursing and I found it too hard to absorb."

We talked about how it 'creeps her out' and how she can't even be in the same room with ashes, not even her own pets. I felt bad for her. I knew; by the look on her face that this was a very uncomfortable subject. Yet, I also could see it was something she wanted to share with me. She said her and her husband had a heated discussion about their pet being cremated and she was afraid she was losing.

I now remembered that she once told me she and her hubby would be cremated when the time came.

"Have you changed your mind?" I asked.

"No it just creeps me out and I can't help it."

"Well Ron and I have our plots already. The fact is we are being buried in a family plot which dictates cremation." I continued, "As a matter of fact, I told Ron that we should consider a brilliant plan I have."

"What is that?" Cheryl asked.

"I think we should be buried in the same Urn, at the same time."

"How would that work?" She questioned with a frown.

"Well whoever goes first would be kept in the Urn until the other one passes." I continued

With, "Then, when the other one goes we would be put in the same Urn together." *Flabbermouth striking again* I said, "The only thing I ask is that no one shakes us up. I don't want something stuck in my mouth that should not be there, especially for eternity."

Cheryl started to laugh so hard, she was snorting. "Oh my gawd," She cried through her snorts. "Chris only you could take something I am afraid of and make me see it in a whole new light."

Hunched over with a stitch in her side and through tears, she repeated, "I am so happy I came for coffee tonight, I just hope I can drive home without the car shaking."

The phone rang disrupting the moment. Her hubby wanted her to go pick up her kids at soccer and go home. She could not even talk to him she was laughing so hard.

"Yep she is on her way," I told him.

"Is everything alright?" He asked.

"Absolutely all is right." I replied.

As I said in the beginning of this story, Cheryl just called. She wanted to tell me she may never fear cremation again, but the vision I left in her head is disturbing to say the least.

My last words before I hung up were, "And you thought the Kamara Sutra left images."

She started to laugh again and I could hear her snorting between. "Only you Chris, only you!"

"Good night, Cheryl."

Chapter Four: The Drinks on Me

Marilyn, a very good friend, was having a bridal shower for her daughter Lynne. The unanimous decision for not having strippers at either the shower or the stag was agreed upon by both the bride and groom. She was not sure however to make the shower fun without the silly parlor games and party favors. So she decided to have the showed at a well-known reputable hotel and local bar. The idea being no one would have to drive home inebriated. This was not a problem for me as I had never been a drinker. My unfortunate childhood memories of drinkers and the fact I took so many pain meds were both strong factors. I did, however, occasionally enjoy one mixed drink that my Stepsister learned to make in Bartending School. The love of cherries was my downfall and the fact the drink had cherries in it was a plus. The drink was called, 'A Cherry Hooker'- cherry brandy and orange juice with 3 cherries impaled on a plastic skewer. I always requested a whole lot more orange juice and a lot less brandy though. It was quite the joke about my heavy drinking.

My kids teased me saying, "If you even open a beer bottle in the same room as Mom, she gets drunk."

Ron said I was a cheap date to say the least. I was looking forward to the night out and figured I would nurse just one drink. Therefore, anyone I didn't know, wouldn't ask 'none of their business' questions. I didn't advertise my 'no' drinking habits as sometimes I found I was defending myself. I was also not familiar with the newfangled drinks that were circulating the bars .I wouldn't say I was a prude, but I was a bit naive.

When I arrived at the hotel, everyone else had already been seated at a table. I knew most of the girls, but there were a couple new faces. We did our usual polite introductions.

Marilyn then asked, "Who wants a drink?"

All hands were flailing in the air and an array of drink names shouted out. Marilyn waved her arms to calm everyone down.

Marilyn said, "I think the late comer should do the honors and place the drink order."

The other guests thought that was a great idea and I of course was the late comer.

"Okay," I said, "What is everyone drinking?"

Marilyn winked at me and smiled, "You'll have to memorize the drink names, and they are not what you are used to hearing. There are so many new drinks nowadays."

"Not a problem I will write them down." Then I asked, "Why don't we just give the order to the waitress?"

Lynne piped up and said, "If you give them to the bartender first, the waitress can just keep filing our orders for the rest of the night it makes more sense that way."

I shrugged, "Okay no problem." I was ready to write," So what's the order?"

I was surprised at the list, but I was assured I had it written down properly. So I hesitantly marched off to the bartender.

Now, I was sitting on a very high stool looking straight into the face of this very handsome, young bartender. Behind me, I could hear giggles, but I didn't pay too much attention. I needed to concentrate on the very unusual drink list. I could feel myself blushing and I thought to myself, oh boy, where was I to start?

I know, I would start with the simple drinks first. Looking down at the list and trying not into the eyes of the handsome bartender, I started.

Leslie, ordered a Screwdriver. With that, the bartender nodded. Carol wanted a Planters Punch again that brought a casual nod. Betty wanted a Slow Screw? Yep that one was okay but now, he began to smile. Lynne, ordered a Slow Screw with a twist? Whew, this was getting a little embarrassing. The bartender didn't even miss a beat he kept mixing and pouring. Now for Cathy's she wanted an Orgasm. By now I was getting a bit flustered and had my face lowered and my hand shielding my eyes.

Now my drink, flabbermouth blurted out, "Do you know how to make a Happy Hooker?"

"No my dear, but I do know how to make a hooker happy." With that, everyone at the table burst out laughing. These wonderful ladies had set me up. The bartender was in on the whole deal. The drinks were indeed genuine drinks, but the girls at the table were not having any of them. The most exotic drink served that night was my Cherry Hooker. Now who other than your friends would love you so much and feel comfortable enough to embarrass you in front of a handsome bartender and still know you love them.

Chapter Five: Happy Mother's Day

Mother's Day was coming and I have always loved getting handmade cards from my hubby Ron. I felt there was so much more love in a handmade card versus a store bought one. Ron was not great at writing love poems in mine, but he always came up with a quote that was both loving and appropriate.

My daughter Christine was going to be on her own for the first time since being newly divorced. Shandra, her daughter was too young to do anything for her on this special day so I thought I would. Since I wrote poetry and knew how to use the computer program to make the cards I would try it. I felt I penned the perfect poem. Not mushy or generic but something that would give her a much needed lift.

I hand painted a picture of wild roses on a demin jacket that she had requested as a gift and then used that picture on the front of her card. After picking out the best font for the poem, I printed it and sealed it in an envelope that I also made. On the front of the envelope, I hand printed 'To My Wonderful Daughter' in calligraphy.

Her father and I then invited her and our wonderful granddaughter over for brunch. After brunch, we exchanged cards. I was so proud. I just knew she would love the card as much as she did her painted jacket. I had a huge smile on my face as she opened it. I winked at Ron who gave me the thumbs up.

All of a sudden, Christine started to laugh. She was laughing so hard she could not speak. Perplexed I took the card from her and read," I know I'm not your mother."

Need I say more? Not a Mother's Day passes that she doesn't remind me of my special Mother's Day card that only 'her mother' could have written. Ron just rolled his eyes and shook his head.

Chapter Six: Painting by the Numbers

I was the unwilling recipient in a devastating hit and run car accident caused by an uncaring, thoughtless drunk driver. That horrendous accident changed my life forever. I was robbed of my careers that I worked so hard for *and* further lowered my already deflated my self-esteem. The damage I sustained led up to my enduring three painful and debilitating back surgeries. The third one involved my having to have my tailbone removed. I needed to find something to do to keep my mind busy and to help me cope with the hideous, unbearable pain.

I was writing more poetry but that was not keeping my mind sufficiently occupied. After attending the pain clinic for the third time my specialist and I discussed what I might do as therapy that would not put any more stress on my spine but help me mentally.

He sat facing me tapping his fingers on his desk. Finally, he said, "Well, Chris, I think you need to find something to do in a reclined position with your knees up."

Flabbermouth blurted out, "Well seeing as I can only have sex so many times a day, I guess I should start looking for something else to do."

I believed the doctor was going to swallow his tongue as he choked, "I knew I should have worded that different as soon as it passed my lips." He was laughing too hard to finish his next sentence smoothly. "Chris, you make my day, I swear, life would be so boring without you."

On my way home from the doctor's I stopped at a craft store. I found a kit that had 6 fabric paints, a sweatshirt and instructions on how to do fabric painting. That was my introduction to the start of my new business 'Painted Originals.' I had never painted anything crafty up until that moment.

Since that fateful day and for the next 20 years, I have taught myself to paint on every medium. I now paint with acrylics and oils on cloth, wood, glass, slate, stone, canvas and walls. God has blessed me with these gifts to help me deal with my daily chronic pain.

As a thank you, I surprised my doctor with a sweatshirt and painted on it his favorite wild animals 'wolves.' Several years later he shared with me that he wore that sweatshirt as often as he could.

He said, "Whenever someone asks me about the art work I would tell them our story." He finished with, "It always makes them laugh."

I came to believe 'laughter is the best medicine' even for a doctor.

Chapter Seven: Where are the Penguins?

Ron had just earned the 'salesman of the year' award at work, and we were going to Florida for a week. Everything included for the week would be paid for. We needed to take only our clothes and toiletries. This was an honor as only the top sales people from Canada and the US would be there. This time of year here in Canada, there was snow up to our wazoo and we would be spending a week in sunny Florida. How cool was that?

The well planned and thorough itinerary was all set out for us. Meeting us at the airport were Ross the president and his wife Gail. They represented one of the biggest Compressed Gas companies in the world. We would be transported from place to place in stretch limos. Our first stop was a beautiful, expensive tropical restaurant for a luxurious luncheon.

Gail asked us, "Would you like to take the scenic route to the hotel?" Adding, "We have a lot to see if there is any interest?"

Ron and I loved to travel and expressed we thought this was a wonderful idea. "Great," she said, "we will drive along the water, sound wonderful?" In unison we all agreed.

This was Ron's first company fully paid vacation. Every detail was perfectly planned for us, we felt energized. The fact we were in the company of the 'big wigs' made the excitement even more exhilarating.

As we were driving along the coastline, I spotted a large mass on the water. All excited I grabbed Ron's arm and shook him. Flabbermouth said, "Ron, Ron look at all the penguins. Oh my gawd I have never seen penguins before let alone so many!"

"Penguins?" Ron quizzed.

"Yes over there can't you see them?"

Gail was laughing so hard saying, "Ron, do you take her out of the house often?"

"No, really, they are right over there!" As I pointed to the feathery mass on the water.

"Shall I tell her or do you want to?"

Ron looked at me very embarrassed and said, "Honey, can we say P E L I C A N S?"

I looked at him as if he was nuts, "Y E S that is w h a t I said."

"N O, what you said was penguins."

Covering my face with my hands, I could feel my face turning red as I muttered, "I am sorry but you knew what I meant."

By now everyone was hysterical.

Gail reached over the front seat and patting my hand said, "That's ok, Chris. I needed a good laugh today and how best to laugh with someone who does it so naturally."

Ron reassured me there wasn't a problem with my flabbermouth moment and I should not be embarrassed.

That night at the festive dinner, on our plates there was a large white envelope containing ample spending money for the week, keys to a Town car and on top of the envelope on my plate was a mini stuffed penguin. Ross and Gail definitely had a great sense of humor. For the rest of the week, whenever possible, someone threw in a penguin remark. All in fun, my friends, all in fun

Chapter Eight: Ticket Anyone?

A wonderful vacation must always come to an end. No matter how long or how far you have gone there is a time to go home. It was one of those times for us. We had a wonderful two-week on a driving vacation with our nine years old son, Doug. Ron loves to drive and does most of it, but occasionally he will ask me to drive while he catches some shut eye.

After being in seven car accidents (none being my fault for those asking), I am a very careful and a slower driver than Ron. When Ron drives, we usually pull out of the driveway and after the initial take-off, we land at our next stop. Anyway, I am not one of those drivers. Therefore, when I was pulled over in Northern Ontario, I was shocked.

Ron softly said, "Be calm you were not speeding so maybe we have a light out or something."

The officer strolled up to the car and peered in my side window, he was peering at a very nervous Chris. I had never been stopped before and I was worried. Very politely, the officer acknowledged Ron, Doug and then me.

He then proceeded to ask," Do you know how fast you were going?"

"Yes sir, I do and I know that if the speed limit is one hundred then I was going slightly under that."

He grinned and said, "I didn't stop you for speeding and yes you are correct." Speaking again he said," I noticed you are from Ontario and may not know the danger of Moose this far north. It is getting dusk and you are heading onto some very winding roads. I just wanted to ask you to slow down a little bit. The Moose roam freely across the roads and they are humongous compared to your car. It would take nothing for one to cause a very serious accident or even death."

I thanked the officer and cautiously drove away. Ron explained to Doug why his mother didn't get a ticket but was still pulled over.

The next day after a good night's sleep, we headed out again. We decided to go the remainder of the way home through the US. It was a shorter route in the long run. Again, Ron decided I should take over driving for a while, he needed a nap. Doug and Ron traded places and Doug rode shotgun with me. It was only about a half hour later we heard and saw the dreaded flashing lights coming up behind me. I looked at my speedometer and everything looked good on my end. "What now?" I said in a panic, fearing the big officer as he approached my car.

"Good morning, officer."

"Good morning, miss; do you know how fast you were going?" He asked as he glanced at Doug in the front seat and Ron lying down in the back.

"Yes sir I do."

"And how fast do you think that was?"

I looked at my speedometer and said, "Fifty miles an hour or very close to it."

"I would like your license and registration please," very politely, he asked.

"May I ask why you stopped me?" Fidgeting for my items in my glove compartment, I then handed him my information.

After checking everything out he said, "I see you are from Canada?"

"Yes sir." Now I was getting worried.

"Tell me again how fast you were going?"

"Well we don't have a mile indicator on my speedometer, so Ron said if I kept the thingy here between these two numbers I would be safe." I explained as I wiggled my finger up and down between the two numbers I was referring to.

"So you are not certain as to your speed?" He snapped.

"Well Ron drives in the US all the time and he said if I keep the thingy right here I would be ok. Where should it be if that is the wrong place?" I nervously and sheepishly asked.

"I don't know. I have never driven a car that has kilometers on it but you were speeding."

"I am sorry sir, but could you tell me where I should keep the thingy to be safe?"

"I don't know what you are talking about," he said.

So I reached over and by his neck pulled his head into the car as far as I could and said, "See I keep it right there." I pointed to the number closest to the fifty mile indicator.

By this time, Ron was stirring in the back seat. He bolted upright at the sight of me with my hand on a police officer's neck. Doug was sitting beside me very quietly, his eyes as huge as saucers.

The officer quickly stood up and replaced his hat as he said," I think maybe you have oversized tires on your car so just try to keep the 'thingy' just under where Ron told you to, and you," as he pointed to Ron, said, "Do up your seat belt." He added," I am only giving you a warning this time but if you get stopped again you will get a ticket."

Just then my sweet supportive, flabbermouth son piped up," You aren't letting her away with it again are you, she got away with it yesterday?"

I smiled and waved as the officer slowly pulled away.

Ron laughed saying," That's my son." Looking at me he scolded," And don't you ever touch another police officer like that. Woman, you could have found yourself in jail."

To this day at seventy one years old I have never received a ticket for speeding.

Chapter Nine: Autopsy Anyone?

I left my surgeon's office in a complete and utter fog and I was so very grateful. He had just told me the test he sent away came back and I *did not* have breast cancer. The liberation is something that cannot be explained in the few moments I have here. But believe me when I tell you I felt as if I had been given a new lease on life. Little did I know, that the next appointment that I had later that day would bring me news just as devastating. I had complained to my surgeon that I was having problems swallowing. Because of the breast cancer scare, he wanted to have my throat checked out. The bad news was I had thyroid cancer. Before ordering surgery, I needed a few more tests.

One of the first things I needed to do was see my cardiologist. I have a valve problem and must be checked before undergoing any kind of procedure. My cardiologist had his practice in the University Hospital, a teaching hospital. When he asked if I would mind if a student doctor sat in on our visit, I had absolutely no reason to say, "No." After almost 35surgeries I was grateful to these teaching facilities. The young man that entered the room with my doctor looked more like a high school student than an intern. My cardiologist was giving the intern the short version of my four inch thick file he held in his hand. The look on the intern's face was one of shock and surprise.

Then getting down to business he said, "My dear Chris, what brings you to see us today?"

Before I had a chance to answer he said, "According to our files you've had a couple scary days."

"Yes it has been a bit of a roller coaster ride," I answered.

"So what's on the agenda?"

Flabbermouth chipped in, "Well on Tuesday I go for an autopsy and then we will have some answers."

"An autopsy? I don't think so."

"Yes. I'm sure it is booked for Tuesday at the Hamilton Hospital."

As I was talking, I watched the look on the intern's face. I was not sure what to make of it. He was wearing a half grin but looked like he was going to burst out laughing. My doctor noticed the same look so he immediately cut in with, "You mean a biopsy right? Because my dear if you were going for an autopsy, a biopsy would *not* be necessary." The three of us started to laugh in unison. I was so embarrassed. My doctor, trying to make me more comfortable, said, "Chris, you are one of a kind." Turning to the intern he said, "You will be one lucky doctor if you have just one patient like her in your entire practice. They both wished me good luck with my autopsy and bid me farewell until next time. I will let you in on a little secret. I came through the cancer surgery and passed on the autopsy.

Chapter Ten: Driving Erotic

By now, most of my readers and fans know I have been in seven car accidents. I know in its self, this is not something to brag about but I can brag that not one of these was my fault.

Ron, a driver most his life, once told me, "A minor accident is like falling off a horse you have to get right back on and ride. If you don't you may never ride again."

Following his advice, I did just that. Once arriving home, I knew he would want a viable explanation for the damage to his brand new company car. I was tremendously upset and as soon as I saw Ron, I started blubbering. He put his arms around me. First making sure I was not seriously hurt. At the same time, he was rubbernecking past me to see the damage. Through my sobs, I was trying to explain what happened. Placing his hands on my shoulders, he led me to the couch and said, "Hon, sit down, take a deep breathe and make some sense. Now until you calm down, I will ask the questions and you need only answer with a yes or no okay?" I nodded yes. "Let's start," he said. "Did you cause the accident?"

"No."

"Did you get his information?"

"Yes."

"Did you call the police?"

"Yes."

"Alright, are you able to tell me what happened now?"

"Yes." I said, drying my eyes and taking a deep breath. "First I am so sorry, honey for the car."

He put his index finger to his lips shushing me, saying, "If you didn't cause the accident it is not necessary to be sorry."

"Thank you." I continued, "I was driving on the 401. In my rear view mirror, I saw a small, yellow, sports car darting in and out of traffic. I was getting nervous as he was tailgating me. I moved over so he could pass. As soon as I could, I pulled off the highway and he followed. Pulling into a fast food parking lot, he followed me there too. Now I was frightfully concerned."

Ron was getting very agitated as I was talking. "So what did he want?" he quizzed.

"I was afraid as he pulled up beside me. He got out of his car and I, being fearful, locked my doors. He thought I was an old friend and when he saw I wasn't he impatiently pulled out of the lot hitting the side of our car."

"What did he say?"

"He didn't say anything, he drove away."

"Did you call the police?"

"Of course I did." I was annoyed at the question. "I used the phone at the fast food place. Luckily, one of the patrons saw the whole thing." I proudly finished with (flabbermouth) "I informed the police he was driving dangerously erotic. I noticed this from the moment he pulled onto the highway and while he was tailgating me. It was especially noticeable when he followed me into the parking lot."

Violently shaking his head in disbelief he said, "Erratic my dear erratic. Not EROTIC. I am sure he was fully clothed without anything hanging out." Still shaking his head he clutched it in his hands, "Oh boy, you probably made the policeman's day with that one." Realizing my stupid blunder, we both laughed at the disturbing sight and the tension was lightened.

Chapter Eleven: Prostitution Indeed

The summer of 1989 we moved into a new neighborhood. We had a lovely house built at the end of the court. The only problem with building a new home is the landscaping has to be done. Ron and I would often drive around the city looking for ideas. Virginia, while at the house getting her hair done, suggested we walk around some of the nicer landscaped areas to get ideas. I was now only able to look and take notes. After my car accident I was not able to help with the labor, as much as I would have enjoyed it. That was up to Ron and our three children. This upset me, I loved gardening and it was a reminder of one more thing I could no longer do. I would however be the one who designed the gardens. This at least kept me involved.

Virginia and I would take a walk each week after her hair appointment. Every once in a while we would stop and admire the landscaping and if the owners were outside we would stop and talk. I am a very chatty person and have no fear of starting up a conversation. I am also quick to pick up on the clues given when someone does not want to be bothered. A few times when we would be on our tours we would get wolf whistles, Virginia would say," well my friend, model or not you still got it." We would laugh but I felt proud of the way I looked, until I remembered the reason I was no longer modeling. Then sadness would wash over me, but only for a flash of a second

The house half way down the block had been built and finished the same time ours was. They had a great deal of landscaping done already. The owner was always out working in the yards. Virginia and I would often stop and talk to him and he shared some very interesting ideas. His wife could be seen just inside the kitchen window, behind the curtains. Within minutes she would demand he go into the house. This happened every time.

I mentioned this to Ron and he said, "Maybe she is jealous of other women talking to her husband."

"Maybe we shouldn't talk to him anymore." I said.

"Don't be silly. I am sure he is a big boy and can handle a little conversation."

"I guess you are right he does have some great ideas, he seems to like to brag about his gardening skills. I have learned a lot from him so far."

"Well then, let him decide if he wants to talk to you and Virginia or not."

"Okay, but I don't want to cause a problem between a hubby and his wife."

Still I decided the next time we went that way we would not go out of our way to stop and talk. Although we had to walk past their house to go to the common post boxes to get our mail so it was unavoidable. As we were passing, he came towards us and asked if he could show us the new pond he was designing?

I said, "Ron will be home in an hour he would love to see it as well could we do it then."

He seemed very pleased to be showing off his handiwork. Ron and I walked down the street after dinner and Roger introduced himself.

He indicated his wife Stella, was busy or she would have joined us. He was happy that two other neighbors wanted to see the pond as well. The five of us exchanged landscaping ideas and we oohed and awed over Roger's designs. We discussed having many new ideas to think about.

As usual I was walking past Roger's and Stella's to get out mail. Roger was not out but Stella was at the side of the house desperately trying to get my attention. I stopped and walked to wards her up her driveway. When I was just a few feet from her, she said, "I don't want you to talk to my husband any more you are distracting him from his work."

I was stunned and just stared at her as she turned her back to me and walked away. On the way home in shock, I mulled over in my head what had just happened. Asking myself, "What the hell was that about?"

When Ron arrived home I told him what occurred. He said, "What did you say?"

"I said nothing I was stunned.

"Well you still have to walk by to get the mail."

"I know. I will handle whatever comes my way." I assured him.

The next day I decided to walk past their house quickly. This way I might go unnoticed. No such luck. Just as I was almost past, Roger called out to me, "Chris come meet my wife Stella." Trying to show I was the better person here, I walked up to wards them and said, "Hello there I see you like to garden as well as Roger." She grunted a hello at me and continued working. Roger excused himself needing to get more mulch. As he left her eyesight, Stella said. "What did I tell you?

I said, "You know Stella, I was just trying to get some ideas for our landscaping and Roger was helpful. I miss being able to help my hubby with these projects since my accident. I am no longer able to bend, kneel or lift."

Very sarcastically she said, "And just what was it you used to do?"

Flabbermouth said, "I was a prostitute!"

Stella could hardly stomp off fast enough and Roger could be heard belly laughing from the side of the house. Roger still says hi and smiles when he sees me, but I haven't see Stella hiding behind the curtains as of late.

Chapter Twelve: A Stitch in Time

On one overly warm Canadian summer day, finding myself home alone and bored. I thought, what a lovely day to spruce up the walls in the guest room. I already had them painted but they looked so very plain. I planned to paint a mural on the one wall, but was undecided on what theme to choose. I remembered putting a roll of wallpaper in the hall closet. After looking at it for several minutes, I finally made a decision. I would cut the pattern out of the paper, making enough border to go around the room just about the height of the window. With a very small pair of cuticle scissors, I started cutting. I was sure it would take me all day. It was painstaking work to cut all the tiny intricate parts. When I was finished, I just knew it was going to look wonderful. The colors and pattern matched the bedspread on the double bed and the lampshade that sat on the light blonde end table. Even the colors in the big-armed chair seemed to pop out nicely. I very carefully took the blinds down being cautious not to hurt myself or strain my already painful back. The stepladder I was using was just the right height so I did not have to stretch. When it was all done, I stood back and admired my creativity giving myself an imaginary pat on the back.

A couple hours later I was walking up our semi-spiral staircase to the upstairs and noticed a corner of the paper over the window had not stuck. I was sure it was not a big deal and decided to fix it immediately. My only dilemma was how to get to it without the ladder. Not a problem! I would just stand on the arm of the chair. It was a big heavy-made chair from a sofa set. It sure looked and felt sturdy enough. So up I went, and then down I came. The descent was much faster than the ascent. I cracked the back of my head on the corner of the nightstand. Blood spurted on the wall, bed and carpet making a pattern in red on one side of the bedroom. I tried on three occasions to stand only to fall down again. On the fourth try, I was successful.

Stumbling into the adjoining bedroom I picked up the phone, pushing buttons until someone answered. I could not see what I was doing, as for reasons unknown I could not open my eyes. I just cried, "Help me, help me." I had no idea who I was talking to. It so happened I reached my friend Lil next door. I could feel the warm sticky liquid running down my neck and back. Scared and unable to open my eyes I headed for the washroom. I collapsed on the hall floor just at the top of the stairs. That is where Lil and Norm found me. No matter how hard I tried I could not open my eyes.

I knew I was in trouble when Norm, (who had once stitched up his own leg when he cut it open with a box cutter) began to shake. It was not long before the ambulance and medical response team where there to take care of me. By now, Lil had assessed and cleaned the area in which I accomplished my stupidity. The beige hall carpet was a different story. It was blood soaked where my head had been lying. Trying to do their jobs and needing to see how badly I was hurt, the EMT's preformed a thorough exam. It was their conclusion I was in shock. After putting my neck in a brace and just before putting me on a backboard one of the EMT's said, "Chris, we need to ask some very important questions. Do you know where you are?"

37

Flabbermouth, "I'm laying right here on the floor in my hall, where the heck do you think I am?"

Lil, laughed and said, "Well she sounds like her old self to me."

We arrived at the hospital and once I was stabilized and the bleeding stopped, the doctor came in to stitch my head. He was about four foot nothing. He dragged the small footstool that was in every hospital room and stepped up on it. Placing his knee on the cot, he leaned over me. His nose almost touching mine as he asked, "Does standing on the arm of a chair with a bad back, sound stupid to you?" I nodded my head and winced as it hurt. "Now what is stupider than that, may I ask?"

Flabbermouth answered, "Me standing on a chair that doesn't have a bad back?"

He was not amused.

Before I was released a nurse came into the room to talk to me.

She said, "I am sorry but I need to ask you a question. The doctor needs to know if your husband did this to you."

Shocked at her question I asked her why she would ask such a thing?

She answered, "The doctor said your husband was very cool to you and refused to hold your hand. He noticed that it was your daughter who was your support and that he spoke to you in a very angry voice."

I started to laugh, "My poor hubby was in Toronto when I fell. He was acting like he did because I did a very stupid thing which could have had major consequences, not just for me but for our whole family."

She smiled and nodded as if she understood.

Doug our son, was working late that night and was not home when all of this occurred, so when he came home and saw me standing at the top of the stairs with my head wrapped in a huge white blood stained bandage and my hair sticking straight up he burst out laughing. I thought he was going to wake the house he was laughing so hard.

"So you think this is funny?" I asked.

"Not at all," he said, "It is flippin hilarious. Remember when you hit me with the garage door? Well I see this as payback time." He could hardly get the words out and he had tears in his eyes.

"I hope your belly hurts from laughing."

"It does but it is so worth it." We both got the giggles then.

For the next few weeks, I was teased unmercifully. Frank, Ron's brother was the worst one. Here are just a few comments, "Anyone want a coffee, tea or a chair?" or "Pass me the butter, salt pepper or the arm of the chair." or "I need some wallpaper hung, anyone have a chair?"

Yes, I learned my lesson.

Chapter Thirteen: Syphilis Remedy

One of the many products I sold was Nutri-Metics a skin care, make-up and supplement line. While visiting Sharon, one of my neighbors, she was complaining about her new glasses causing a very painful and red rash on her nose. It seemed she was sensitive to the plastic used in the nose piece. I was sure I had received a new flier that very morning advertising an exciting new product, an Aloe Vera based cream. I ran home to get the information and phone number for our head office to get more information.

Sharon and I scoured over the ingredient list and information and it was indeed something she could use. The information sheet was vague on the date of availability, so I thought I would call head office immediately.

"Good afternoon, Nutri-Metics, may I help you?"

"Yes please, I am Chris Hannon one of your consultants from Paris Ontario"

"Yes Chris, I know who you are, you are speaking to Diane. How can I help you today?"

"I see in your new flyer you have a wonderful new product that is Aloe Vera based and I was wondering when it might be available."

"Chris, at this time we only have samples, what do you need it for?"

"Well I have a customer who has a great need. She has tried everything on the market and most things react to her skin in a negative way. I thought this would be the answer to her problem."

"Can you tell me what her problem is and we can go from there."

"Sure –flabbermouth strikes - she has syphilis of the nose."

"Excuse me!" Diane sounded shocked at my answer.

"She has syphilis of the nose from her glasses." As I was speaking Sharon was anxiously waving her hands in the air. I put my hand up to let her know I was getting information, but she was shaking her head violently and finally said "Psoriasis not syphilis."

"Hello Chris, are you still there?" Now embarrassed, I acknowledged I was. I could hear the laughing on the other end of the phone and a very apologetic Diane. "I am so sorry but I have never been asked for a product to help heal syphilis of the nose before."

Sensing my discomfort and being the professional she was she assured me she would not share this conversation with anyone else. Before I hung up we had a good laugh and Sharon laughed too. We did however accomplish my goal and Diane happily sent out samples to us. By the way yes the product worked.

Chapter Fourteen: Nuns Bean Embarrassed

One afternoon when grocery shopping with my young grandson Ronnie. He was amusing himself by repeating some sayings he had heard from others or he would make up his own as we picked up items. One box of cereal he spotted, he started singing the alphabet song. Strolling in the cheese aisle caused him to chime, "cheese please," over and over again as he picked up the packages we needed.

By the time we got to the canned goods I was sure we were home free. But the next row we walked down brought the biggest surprise. The canned beans! As if he was auditioning for Canadian Idol he broke into song. "Beans, beans the musical fruit, the more you eat the more you toot."

We both started to laugh as he finished with a little dance.

Without a beat Flabbermouth added a second verse. "Tweddle de dee, Tweddle de dumb, in your mouth and out your bum."

My grandson started to giggle but abruptly stopped and looked as if he saw a ghost. Sensing his discomfort I turned and looked behind me, where I was face to face with two nuns who were trying very hard not to laugh. I was stumbling for the proper words to apologize, when the elder nun said, "I have not heard that little ditty since I was a child, it certainly brought back some great family memories. Well except for the second verse." With that she started to laugh easing my embarrassment.

Ronnie could not wait to get home to tell daddy and mommy that Grammies, did it again. He rolled his eyes in embarrassment as he told his 'Nun' story.

About the Author

I am Chris, a 71-year-old medically retired lady who lives in Woodstock, On. CA. I have 3 wonderful children a daughter and 2 sons. Also in our family are our sonin-law and our daughter in law both whom I love as if they were my own. I have two grandchildren, a thirty-one year-old granddaughter and an eleven year-old grandson. Ron and I have been married 52 years. Until a major car accident 43 years ago that took away my livelihood, I worked as a hairdresser, makeup artist and model.

After listening to my hairdressing, stories a million times, my family suggested I write a book about them. I have written poems for as long as I can remember. But writing a novel was foreign to me. I never thought it was possible. Having less than a grade 9 education made it seem out of my reach. Others convinced me that if I told my stories in print as I did verbally they would definitely be worth reading. Therefore, "A Hairdresser's Diary" was in the making.

I am a self-taught artist. I started approximately 20 years ago. I first began painting on clothing, moving on to murals, wood pieces and stone and finally graduating to canvas. I use both acrylics and oils. This started out to be therapy and still is my way of dealing with daily chronic pain

My other published books are:

A Hairdresser's Diary

A Hairdresser's Diary: Scissors Retired

A Cut above Discrimination

Say it with a Poem

There are 3 others in the works.

I can be found at Amazon- in both soft covered and e books, Kindle, Kobo, LULU, Barnes & Noble, Smashwords, Nook – also in e book form.

www.ingramcontent.com/pod-product-compliance
Lightning Source LLC
Chambersburg PA
CBHW060632030426
42337CB00018B/3318